MW00843316

to:

from:

tweet nothings

The Lighter Side of Twitter

Compiled with an Introduction
by Suzanne Schwalb

Illustrations by Margaret Rubiano

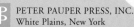

PETER PAUPER PRESS, INC.
White Plains, New York

Designed by Margaret Rubiano

Copyright © 2010
Peter Pauper Press, Inc.
202 Mamaroneck Avenue
White Plains, NY 10601
All rights reserved
ISBN 978-1-59359-777-1
Printed in China
7 6 5 4 3 2 1

Follow us on
Twitter @peterpauperpres

Visit us at www.peterpauper.com

tweet
nothings

The Lighter Side
of Twitter

introduction

Welcome to Twitter, the microblogging phenomenon that's keeping families, friends, and followers around the world connected through those "quick, frequent" 140-character, er, Tweets that answer the question "What are you doing?" Whether describing one's bran muffin, confirming a Tweetup, frienda-paloozing, Tweeting from a trade show, or instigating a revolution, Twitter has

become the 21st-century's *vox populi.* "Soon everyone will know everyone else," as someone recently Tweeted. And frequented as it is by fun and funny people, Twitter can be hilarious. Here is a compilation of some of our favorite broadcasts from the Hive Mind, from quibbles and bits to dispatches from domesticity. The Bard once said, "Brevity is the soul of wit." How Tweet it is!

What the hell is this thing? I'm supposed to tell you what I'm doing? Why would I tell you what I'm doing? What are YOU doing?
@larry_david

" love the happy laundry day accident of putting on what you think is unmatching, and then realizing you look more stylish than usual. "

@tinafey

Day 5 of my Colombia trip, and I'm out of clean underwear. But there's no way I'm "going commando." I oppose U.S. military intervention.

@adamisacson

I have boxes all over my house for moving, but so far the only thing I have packed is my cat, eight times.
@baileygenine

I should get my interns to fill up super soakers with coffee and just hose me down regularly.
@Agent_M

"My morning just fell on the floor butter side down."
@sniffyjenkins

" My hotel bathroom has a Regenerative Care Bar, a Ginseng Exfoliant Lozenge, and a Clarifying Body Bullet. Will trade for soap. "

@scottsimpson

Thank you Crate and Barrel for your clean and delightful public restrooms. A great place to chat up new friends while I bathe in your sink.
@robhuebel

“I can’t take a mental health day so I’m dressing like I’m on one.”

@bliccy

Praying my parents don't insist on dragging me to Mass this morning. Oh. Right. Okay, that probably won't work. @cleversimon

I can't believe
it's almost time
to ignore the
lawn again.
@awryone

Two day weekends
no longer suffice
for my expanding
leisure needs.
@badbanana

"i shaved today and now i've got wicked phantom beard." @cluckcluckers

If only I could Tweet from my dreams to help me figure out what the hell was going on in there when I wake up.
@adtothebone

When u r in the bathroom & can hear the boy banging something in one room & the puppy chewing something in another, then u know real fear.
@MRSMOLTZ

"Just hired an emotional Sherpa to carry my ego to the top of Mt Hollywood."

@michael_bay

Last night I explained Twitter as "A bunch of people talking to themselves and once in a while, someone answers." Yeah I'm proud of myself.
@myracles

Back from church.
During communion,
Tiny yelled that she
"didn't get a crouton."
This is why we never
go there.
@MamitaMojita

"Had to pay taxes this year, so I made the check out to AIG."
@CathleenRitt

Kitten pirates, always committing cuteiny.
@AinsleyofAttack

"Glitter glue everywhere. It looks like a fairy exploded." @amazingsoup

my girls got their american girl dolls' ears pierced today. next thing you know the dolls will be getting tattoos.
@chumworth

" Oh. It's a TELE-conference. Cool. I'll need about 20 minutes to shave, stow my bindle, and shoo my cats and companions from the boxcar. "
@hotdogsladies

I try to get to class early and play "How Long Can I Keep Adjacent Seats Open Just By Looking Unpleasant?"
@phyllisstein

My last pedicure client was pregnant and TEN DAYS overdue. And there I was, sitting right in the splash zone.
@expat_erin

“I am astonished that 33 people took the time to review the cheapest letter opener at Staples. Best so far = one line: 'it's a letter opener'”

@hodgman

I feel a tremor in the Force. No, actually it was just my special lunch burrito. My bad.
@darthvader

The problem with marrying someone with intimacy issues is that when I give the silent treatment, he's relieved.
@hoosiergirl

I'm so committed to going green that I've actually started recycling ex-boyfriends.
@Aimee_B_Loved

"What up, WebMD? Whaddya mean 'No results found' for stigmata?"

@nictate

It wasn't funny at the time, but now I can look back on it and drink.
@fireland

@Xerox914: Don't tell anyone about the confidential information I've been copying. Or the body parts. They're for your eyes only. For now. @BadPeggyOlson

"Wait, remind me again, which road is paved with bad intentions? My GPS software seems to be out of date. **@hotheadred**"

Disneyland tip:
Skip the facepainting.
Never pay $17 for
anything that can
be cried off.
@jaboud

❝ At organized–
sports–themed toddler
birthday party. My kid
is definitely the goth
in this group. **❞**
@zeldman

Maintaining a beard is like taking care of a dog that you wear on your face.
@tehawesome

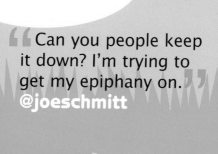

My colon hurts.
Probably because I
followed it with an
apostrophe and a
parenthesis. :'(
@katefeetie

was asked to take
baby's shoes off at
airport. kept mouth
shut. somehow.
@JohnRossBowie

"Multitasking's gonna be the death of me one day — but it'll have to be a day when I have nothing else going on."

@kitson

Coupons in cat litter?
I don't care how long
it takes, marketing
genius. I will find you
and you will perish.
@trelvix

"While babysitting…
'Okay kids, how about
a story?' 'YES!,' they
cried, 'tell us every–
thing you know
about vampires!'**"**
@mhawks

Realizing that just telling my in-laws that I look at porn all day is probably less trouble than actually explaining my creative output.
@bcompton

"My cousin is about to deliver a baby within the next few minutes. I know this because she just updated her Facebook status."

@apelad

i count my blessings
every single day. 1.
the internet. 2. cats
@LILWAYNESWORLD

Life is like walking through a funhouse. It's dark, people are pushing, and you can't turn around. You just follow the cracks of light.
@johncmayer

"wondering how a water bottle with the tagline 'trickled through mountains for centuries' can have an expiration date of next year. whut. "
@LucyRcardo

Knowing what I know now, I would still have devoted my entire childhood to the Atari 2600.
@michaelianblack

Sitting in the back yard, drinking green tea and staring at the newly planted vegetable garden. Damn it feels good to be a gangsta.
@luckyshirt

"A journey of a thousand miles begins with a single step."
Step One: Liquor Store
@MODAT

"Carnies are
people too."
@mikedoe

According to the crime dramas I watched tonight, 1 in every 5 FBI agents is a sexy Latina with a dark past.
@Jessabelle207

That we use a freakish, pagan bunny wielding an egg-basket to teach children about God is pretty funny. On the other hand, these LOLcats.

@NOTcwalken

"My exes play hard
to get rid of."
@pagecrusher

"Of course I missed you. I'm just saying I use a lot less Febreze when you're gone."
@abigvictory

" Dr. Seuss should have written a book called 'Oh, The Places You'll Settle For!' "

@joeschmidt

Dear Inner Child:
What's the matter?
Why are you crying?
Is it because I like
broccoli now? Use
your words!
@zolora

"trying to figure out how i should spend my remaining 18 extra Weight Watchers weekly value points. Eat like a man or drink like a fish?"

@owenburke

People of Brazil: what do you have against hair? Why is your pain threshold so high? Watch tomorrow to see what I'm talking about.
@TheEllenShow

Oh no! My local
Curves is closing!
And during Girl Scout
Cookie season
too! Aack!
@robcorddry

@TheWaltWhitman:
With your obvious devotion to illegal drugs perhaps it behooves us to ponder the true meaning of "Leaves of Grass"?
@Edgar_Allan_Poe

Left my window down when I stopped to pick up anti-depression meds from the pharmacy. It rained. Ha ha.
@SeoulBrother

I can hear my hair going grey.
@pheend

> Had no wifi all day. Couldn't communicate. Missed you all. It was like the Dark Ages. Just without all the disease and oppression. Hold me.
>
> **@paulfeig**

You guys are the best strangers a guy like me could not know.
@DieLaughing